HOW NOT TO BE A VICTIM

VITAL CHALLENGES FROM MISSION ENGAGE YOUTH

Fr James Grant

Connor Court Publishing

The Father James Grant Foundation empowers youth to become powerful assets for themselves and for business through its support and mentoring programs "Mission Engage" and Mission Engage X".

These programs are based in many different business locations and aim to provide real employment pathways for young people otherwise at risk of long-term unemployment and disadvantage. Tailored to the participating business, the Mission Engage Program provides disengaged youth with the necessary skills, training and confidence to improve their employability, their lives and supercharges the positive impact they have on the business.

Most commonly, the program works with 16-22-year-old Australians without a clear vision for their future and who's school, sporting and social experiences have failed to inspire confidence or a strong sense of self. We believe in individual determination and success.

www.fatherjamesgrantfoundation.org

For Stephanie Mignanelli

In gratefulness for her hard work and patience
and her own personal example of resilience and strength

With special thanks to Belinda and Debra
the heart and soul of Crown

Published in 2018 by Connor Court Publishing Pty Ltd

Copyright © James Grant 2018

All rights reserved. This book contains material protected under International and Federal Copyright Laws and Treaties. Any unauthorised reprint or us of this material is prohibited. No part of this book may be reproduced or transmitted in any form by any means, electronic or mechanical, including photocopying, recording, or by an information storage and retrieval system without express written permission from the publisher.

Connor Court Publishing Pty Ltd
PO Box 7257
Redland Bay QLD 4165, Australia

sales@connorcourt.com
www.connorcourtpublishing.com.au
Phone 0497-900-685

ISBN: 978-1-925826-24-1

Cover design: Maria Giordano

The front cover photo: shutterstock

Printed in Australia

FOREWORD

In my review of Father James Grant's 2017 book, *Keeping the Faith: The Battle for Australian Catholicism*, I unhesitatingly remarked that "the Catholic Church in Australia is very fortunate to have Father James in its ranks... the Vatican needs more in the mould of Father James and, frankly, less in the mould of Pope Francis." In that book, Father James offered a clear-eyed assessment of the challenges facing the Catholic Church, the failings of Church leadership in meeting those challenges, and courageously declared what the Church needs to do to rediscover its purpose and how it can contribute to help make Australia a safe, secure and prosperous country.

In his latest book, *How not to be a victim: vital challenges from the mission engage program*, Father James offers another clear-eyed assessment – this time not merely about a religious institution but about an entire generation of Australians that have accepted attitudes and traits that hold them back from flourishing. Father James does not approach the subject as an academic writing in the abstract, but as a man and a Catholic priest who has witnessed the problems first hand of people who embrace victimhood status and has seen how "non-judgementalism" has unsurprisingly not inspired people to be a better version of themselves.

The question at the core of Father James discussion is the question of freedom. Pulling down the legislative restrictions on our freedoms is fundamental to human flourishing. Individual autonomy is inseparable from the concept of dignity, and protecting the legal freedoms of Australians should be amongst the highest priority of parliamentarians.

But this is not the end of the story. What remains is what happens to society when the culture forgets the fundamental lessons and morals that have ordered Western societies for centuries, such as honour, self-responsibility and self-discipline, delayed gratification, eschewing resentment by appreciating what we have, perseverance and the dignity of work, and in particular, the kinds of work that are too often seen as "not worth doing".

When these virtues are lost people have lost freedom in another sense. You are not necessarily free if you have enslaved yourself to self-destructive traits and desires. For instance, you might live in a society where you are legally permitted to consume illicit drugs, but it is less clear you are really "free" if you develop an addiction and become a dysfunctional person.

This is the distinction between ancient and modern liberty, as popularised by the Swiss-French liberal activist and writer Benjamin Constant, where the idea of ancient liberty is derived from the observations of Aristotle, Augustine, and Aquinas. Aristotle and Aquinas saw man as by nature a social creature, and absent of culture and tradition, a person was not a fully formed human. Aristotle wrote that "the city is prior to the family and the individual" to explain how the whole precedes the parts. To use another metaphor, without the body, the limbs of a person are not viable.

The basic idea is that liberty depends on people being educated in virtue, and this comes from being formed and situated within a community that is ordered towards "the good" – or the Platonic *logos*, being the ultimate object of knowledge and from which things that are just gain their usefulness and value. A similar concept later came to be associated with Christ.

Some have argued that a problem with the modern conception of liberty is that it has in turn liberated man of cultural institutions and moral forces that would impose obligations on people to regulate themselves in order to have the "good life".

How not to be a victim is an increasingly timely and necessary work. Fortunately, Father James does not approach this issue in dense philosophical terms, but as a man and an active Catholic priest who has seen the consequences over and over again, and in clear terms recognises the timeless ideas and virtues that need to be reemphasised to ensure no more generations of Australians deny themselves the good life.

-- Morgan Begg is a research fellow at the Institute of Public Affairs

CONTENTS

Introduction		10
1	Your Responsible	18
2	The world owes you nothing	23
3	Your Great Advantage: Australia	27
4	Don't Talk DO	30
5	Walk Through The Door	34
6	Care Less To Succeed	38
7	Freedom and The Importance of You	42
8	Small Steps – Lasting Impact	45
9	No Failure – No Growth	48
10	Find the Gap	52
11	There is no such thing as Genius – Just bloody hard work	55
12	Creating and Sustaining Energy	60
13	Cultivating Excellence	64
14	Black Holes: Drugs, Alcohol and Crime	70
15	Dead end Thinking	74
16	The Tricky God Question	78
17	Kitchen Sink to Michelin Chef	81
18	Seizing Adversity	85
19	Worrying About Yourself	89
20	The Immaturity of Feeling Offended	93
21	Your Culture	96
22	Take the Long Way Home	99
23	From Devotee to Distinction	102
About the Author		104

INTRODUCTION

ASKING THE HARD QUESTIONS?

I know an older person, who is very attached to the idea that life is strongly about helping others. This lady works on a soup kitchen and can be regularly found on Melbourne's streets handing out hot dogs, soup and other food items to Melbourne's homeless in the middle of the night. From time to time this lady's compassion extends to bringing homeless people into her house, giving them a bed, a shower, clothing and small personal items.

The outcome of such actions has not been great. She has been robbed regularly, physically threatened and verbally abused. To this point in time she has had jewellery stolen, televisions, microwaves, cash, watches and phones. She has even come home to finding her full-size refrigerator removed. In my view she has been lucky not to find herself in hospital. When challenged about these events she will note, "I try to be non-judgemental and believe what people tell me."

What am I supposed to make of such a comment and such as series of events from an otherwise intelligent person?

Judgement and Truthfulness are human characteristics that seem to be in short supply in modern Australians and two characteristics that weigh upon this situation as well. Do I feel that she is doing a wonderful thing, that the good she does will outweigh the often bad results? Will I tell her to keep risking her personal safety by inviting little known people into her house and relying totally on their goodwill? Or will I tell her the truth of what I really think, that compassion and a desire to help others cannot be undertaken if it risks personal safety and financial security?

None of the things I had to say to this lady were to be accepted she continues to invite people into her home and continues to be robbed and threatened at regular intervals.

But the question here is much deeper than a risky blind spot shown by a good-natured woman. The deeper question is can we ultimately give any help to others who are not only unwilling to help themselves, but who are living by a set of philosophies that are designed to keep them repeating and re-living dependent lifestyles that will never allow change or growth. Of course, the brutal truth is that the homeless individuals and this lady are both locked in a depressing Groundhog Day in which nobody changes, nobody grows and nobody really lives. In relying on nightly charity, I commit myself to a form of dependence. In believing that somehow my compassion can change lives, without seeing such changes makes me also a dependant on a philosophy that doesn't work. Both these people are victims but shockingly they are both victims by choice!

Our Television sets are full of examples of compassionate people, those who help at wayside chapels, or those Television Advertisements that ask us to part with our money for any number of good causes. Yet, is it the case that anybody asks the hard questions. Yes, it is good to be open, compassionate and non-judgemental to people who come asking for food in centres. But, the hard question is how did they get here, what decisions and actions led them to the outcome of being homeless. What part did drugs or alcohol or failing to finish school or not wanting to find a job have to play in this result? And even more brutally, if other decisions had been taken would we now have a homeless person standing in front of us?

Overwhelming, the hard truth is that bad decisions, lazy actions, a lack of drive or an unwillingness to try have led to these difficult circumstances. This does not mean that condemnation should result but only hard questions and a willingness to change behaviours will be able to lead to different results.

Individuals who are not challenged to change are actually the ones condemned to endless days of no future or hope. When we fail to include any judgement or challenge to change, we are fundamentally disrespectful to that person. All we are doing is condemning them to a way of life that is completely incompatible to a meaningful life. As Jesus Christ himself noted "I came so that people may have the fullness of life". He did not say, I came so that you may survive, tread water or live a life consumed with little more than the pleasures of the moment! The lady who continues to bring people home, gives them free supplies and then finds they steal from her is not helping anyone, including herself. She absolves them of responsibility for their lives and she absolves herself from alleviating misery as she only contributes to more if it occurring.

A doctor that does not challenge their patients to change their lives is not acting as a doctor at all. A doctor who does not challenge the smoker, the drinker or overweight patient doesn't have the best interests of the individual at heart. The disrespect in these instances is severe because this doctor believed no change is possible. This is not to suggest all people will follow a doctor's proposal but not to ask the hard questions is a dereliction of duty and purpose.

Alcoholics and drug users may take years to accept that their lives are a mess, but there is no possibility of change and new life if those around them already accept that nothing can be done. This is perhaps the greatest addiction: to buy into the idea that fate has sealed their life and future and that their own self destruction cannot be overcome.

At "mission engage" our experience and philosophy centres on hard and challenging questions. We do not accept that non-judgementalism is the way to change lives, indeed we consider it to be a form of indifference to the struggle of others. All participants of "mission-engage" are held to a standard of conduct and truthfulness about their own lives. How can any of us learn from experience unless we are told that we can and should change?

WHAT IS A VICTIM?

Everywhere in modern Australia the cry of the victim can be heard loudly and clearly. If you are to visit our Judicial system you will hear a familiar set of excuses pushed out before a magistrate all designed to highlight the victimhood of the individual before the court.

Almost all of their excuses centre on the idea that's it's not my fault: yes, I stole the car or robbed the house, but this can be explained by my poor childhood. This can be justified by the absence of a mother or the violence of a father or the inadequacy of parents in general. Additionally, the corrupted or unfair role of police will also often be highlighted. Designed to downgrade the role of the alleged offender, this suggests that this individual suffers from personal and environmental circumstances over which they have little control.

In a more broader sense this trend towards victimhood can be found in many people who appear to have had little go wrong with their lives at all. This broader victimhood is more than a sense that I have an individual enemy, someone who tried to harm me (perhaps a boss at work that refuses to promote me) but has blossomed for many people into a broad sense of victimhood which has become a philosophy of life where my place within the world is now permanently damaged or attacked.

We can see this most clearly in the fields of sexuality, race and religion. "All men are bastards", or "all white men are angry and controlling", "all blacks are lazy" and "all Catholic priests are paedophiles." The list of such negative stereotypes are endless, but only in comparatively recent times do we see more and more people living within them. These ideas make you a victim, for such ideas debilitate you and stop you changing and developing into a better person.

In my own career I have seen this psychological victimhood play out in many individuals and even within various professions. For many years as a school Chaplain I encountered angry and bitter middle-aged women who although they were comparatively successful felt betrayed by a system they claimed had lied to them and more broadly felt betrayed by men who had allowed this system to flourish. These women were usually characterised as a group of young professionals who had bought into an idea that "career" was everything, it was to a career that women should look for status, acceptance, creditability and internal reward. The cost of such a focus was that many of these women had worked long hours and neglected relationships. They had failed to find partners and had not considered childbirth until biological restrictions made this difficult. To awaken in your early 40's to a realisation that with no partner and without children, the goal of your own family life may be diminishing is certainly confronting. Nevertheless, is it really the case that a "system" that pushes female careers is to blame? and is it accurate to conclude that the "authors" of this system are men who have corrupted women's true natures?

Fundamentally, a truth not considered by all those who feel disillusioned by what has occurred is their lives is a failure to consider their own choices. The choice to pursue career above family was freely taken. Certainly the full costs may not have been considered but the truth remains that no "system" or other individuals constructed the world view that would ultimately disappoint and fail to satisfy.

At this point we can see one of the seductions of the trend to victimhood. Suffering has been elevated to a symbol and measure of the person who is now a victim, but no distinctions may be drawn between psychological or physical suffering or indeed between that which is self-inflicted or that which is fortuitous.

In many cases, the accidents and twists of fate may now

be attribute to "hidden systems" or hidden organisations or associations such as "governments'" who are directly responsible or must be held accountable for solutions. The widely proclaimed supplication "the government should do something about this" is the result of a whole society moving unthinkingly towards victimhood status.

In reality, this new form of thinking, now highly prevalent in Australian life, asserts that once suffering is voiced and victimhood declared, the individual is no longer responsible for the outcomes of life. Responsibility, psychologically and morally can now be shifted to other individuals or more commonly other groups of people or organisations or indeed to "systems" or governments.

The rise of the victim has critical and severe consequences for individuals who accept this type of thinking without consideration. It has blighted the lives of multitudes of Australians. It has made people powerless, indifferent to self-improvement, depressed, listless and ultimately apathetic to the needs of anyone except themselves.

The Mission Engage program takes a different view. We do not accept victimhood as a valid philosophy for the individual. We do not see young Australians as people imprisoned in their circumstances, incapable of change. We see no advantage in a claim of victimhood and we do not accept the statements and conversations that come from individuals locked into this way of thinking.

Mission Engage unashamedly sees the individual as responsible for their own life. For those involved in the Mission Engage program, change and new futures are based on the central idea that individual's control, the thoughts they think, the circumstances they accept and the actions they take.

1

YOUR RESPONSIBLE

The single greatest issue facing the Western World is not economic, it's not relations between men and women, it's not refugees, climate change, unemployment or the breakdown of families. The greatest problem, the one affecting perhaps 90% of modern society is the inability of individuals to take responsibility for their own lives. This is a completely lost art, not taught by our schools, not encouraged by our institutions and not enforced by our Justice system. It is not emphasised in our places of worship or even in our families. You are responsible for the conduct of your life.

When I listen to gamblers comment on the reasons they have lost money, overwhelming people blame the gaming venue, "the venue took my money, the venue seduced me through free drinks, the venue removed the clocks, they had flashing lights and noises that confused me" – all of these comments are based on the most common assumptions underlying many of our belief systems: I am a helpless victim is the face of outside forces. It's not my fault, nobody could resist such behaviour, the government needs to do something about this! Of course, if you mention to individuals with gaming issues that nobody forced them into a gaming establishment, they are usually surprised. Gaming venue staff do not await you as you pass by compelling you with baseball bats to enter their buildings. The often-forgotten truism about such human behaviour is that I chose to undertake a behaviour, I chose to walk on the gaming floor, it was my freewill and the exercise of my freewill that caused me to start gambling. Now certainly this exercise of freewill is often unconsidered and not reflected upon beforehand and certainly there may be other influences, such as pressure from friends that encouraged me along the journey. Nevertheless, the key component of action still resides with the individual: you chose this course of action and you must deal with the consequences.

No learning, change, improved behaviour or sense of self-worth can commence or develop until this fundamental truth is acknowledged and claimed "I am responsible for my own actions!"

The inability to take responsibility for your actions has serious personal consequences. Not to take responsibility for your life, for your actions is to effectively turn yourself into a powerless person. That is the risk of not taking responsibility for your life. If you cannot recognise your responsibility to acknowledge your behaviour and fight to change things, then in essence you acknowledge yourself to be an unfree person, whether its gambling, drugs, alcohol, a bad relationship, a bad friendship group or constantly blaming your parents for your circumstances then you are only admitting that you are a slave to these things – moreover, worse than a person denied freedom you have taken your own freedom away!

The greatest gift we have as humans is our freewill. We have the ability to decide a viewpoint or decide an action. And we also have the ability to hand over our lives and our strengths to something or someone else. When people tell you they cannot resist certain behaviours like drugs, or drinking or criminality, they are only telling you a partial truth. Yes, they may be powerless but they are made powerless by themselves!

Of course, will power and strength of character is like physical fitness, it needs to be cultivated and trained. We cannot just produce will power if we have never used it in the past and if we have never acknowledged the need to use it often.

I well remember a case in my own life where for many years I did not have the strength of character to do and say what I should have. Of course, there are reasons for this, and the greatest is that acting on your will power will normally involve a cost. In this instance a great friend of mine for over 25 years had become involved in a relationship with a married person. For a good twelve months I said nothing, afraid of upsetting my friend. However, I noticed each time we met how unhappy they were. How the passion seemed to have gone out of their life and how they seemed trapped opting for a second-class form of life that always depended on the will and arrangement of others. Finally, I decided to express what I really thought, not only the difficulties of inserting yourself into the lives of others, but mostly the cost that this unfulfilled lifestyle was taking upon my friend. A joyless lifestyle of secret and unfulfilled meetings and the physical and emotional cost that this was plainly taking on my friend. Yet I heard all the usual arguments, this was love, it was the "real" thing and it was felt in a way that couldn't be lost and couldn't be broken. In the end I just couldn't give the approval to this situation that my friend seemed to require. The cost for me has been severe, a 25-year friendship has ended, pain and hurt has occurred on both sides. I can only believe that upholding my values was the best thing I could have done for my friend. Perhaps they do not agree, but I do not believe in supporting and upholding devalued and corrupted lives especially when they are the lives of my friends.

Willpower is something that you control always but there will be a cost. Many of our fellow Australians live devalued lives, these are lives that are afraid to speak up because they fear ….losing a friendship, losing a job, losing a promotion. Many things will challenge our lives, the great question is what will you do? Will you adapt to things you know to be wrong? Will you say nothing in the hope of not being noticed? Or will those around you get a glimpse of what you are really made of.

In most cases of right and wrong nobody will know of your decisions….except one person…yourself!

I meet hundreds of people every day, the saddest are those who choose not to stand up for their values. This situation I wouldn't wish on anyone because it is a decision to not act. It's a decision to live life less than its God-given fullness, it is a decision to betray yourself.

Exercising your will power is the most difficult of all actions, yet ultimately this is the thing that allows you to stand undisturbed when others give in and diminish their own lives. Upholding our own values is always the basis of growing in vision and ultimately making a difference to others.

2

THE WORLD OWES YOU NOTHING

The brutal reality is that life is not fair. In fact, for some people life is even worse, its cruel, harsh and short. If we are prepared to look we can see this reality everywhere. Some people are born with severe intellectual and physical handicaps, some people suffer great hardship because of accidents or disease. Some parents lose beloved children at early ages. The list of human suffering and despair is endless, yet this is one thing we all have in common: we will all suffer.

What we make of that suffering and how we master its consequences are the great questions of life. It is also the great symbols of what you will do with your own life. Human beings have come up with many responses to life's difficulties. Some imagine it is all an illusion, some put their hope in technology, science and medicine, some put their hope in political systems to balance this unfairness, others hope that future genetics or racial purity will somehow solve the dilemma.

Most Australians however, will have none of these reactions. More likely is a response that recognises the truth of our circumstances but then proceed to ignore its consequences. You can hear this clearly in the way we often talk about our lives. "I deserve better than this", "Why did this happen to me", "my parents don't understand me", "If I win Tattslotto this will solve all my problems", "If I meet Mr/Mrs Right I will be happy", "I will join a gym next year and get fit". New year's resolutions are often based on fixing a problem or unfairness in our lives. The truth is we then proceed to do nothing about these circumstances. We float back to a position that suggests change is impossible as these things belong in a "too hard basket!"

One of television's most popular series is a British serial now widely copied in differing countries throughout the world. "Who do you think you are" is based on tracking down the ancestry of local identities and revealing to them the nature of their ancestor's lives, both good and bad. The reaction of the chosen individuals is always revealing, for those who discover significant individuals in their past, expression of pride and gratefulness are normal. For those who find murderers, adulterers, cowards or criminals it seems shame and a determination to redeem or excuse their behaviours is standard.

Undoubtably this series proves one thing beyond doubt, these ancestors who were not a direct influence upon our lives have done little to inform our current lives. Having a famous or notorious ancestor does nothing to tell me anything about who I am. My current life is not shaped by the 'convicts' in my family history, for I know nothing of them and didn't follow their example. In the same way, the goodness of past relatives, unknown to me cannot have shaped my own response to my current world or any behaviours within it.

Certainly, immediate family, parents and grandparents can be significant impactors on our own lives but our relationships to past genetics, nationality or tribal groupings are extremely tenuous. "My Warrior" status might be formed by my parents but certainly not by a genetic connection to Genghis Khan or Erwin Rommel. Indeed, Rommel's son Manfred deserted from military service, entered local government and was noted for his tolerant and liberal works.

If we are to remove the 'myths' of genetics, family grouping, race and cultural markings we still see that overwhelmingly the response of each of us to an 'unfair world' must be one of our making. Importantly, we must stop pretending that something particularly unfair is being done to us. It's not! All of us will encounter random suffering and incomprehensible events.

The response of some people will always be a selfish one. I've got to get what I can before my life is over - in extreme cases these are the individuals found looting in the aftermath of bushfires or natural disasters. Yet, there is another way, for some this may have a Christian foundation, for others it's just done from a realisation that its 'right' for them. This path suggests that focusing on others, helping them or providing encouragement diminishes our own fears and worries. With concern no longer focused on ourselves, I can focus on the 'good' of a particular outcome. How can I make this better for others, my family and friends? How can any personal loss I feel become a benefit to others? Whatever pain, frustration or trouble I may experience can be turned into a source of strength by turning our attention to the service of others.

Service to others acknowledges that there is a world beyond ourselves filled with people who are also suffering and have dealt with worse than the things that befall us. We are not special individuals when we sit and lament our circumstances – we are special when we determine to be known by our actions for others.

- "Whatever you do to the least of my brother you do to me." (Jesus Christ)
- "The best way to find yourself is to lose yourself in the service of others." (Gandhi)
- "The life of a man consists not in dreaming dreams but in active charity and service." (Henry Longfellow)

3

YOUR GREAT ADVANTAGE: AUSTRALIA

The vast majority of Australians are proud to be Australians and proud of our history. A 2018 research poll found that 76% of Australians are proud of their history and 87% are proud of being Australian. This is an enormous advantage for young Australians as they make their way in the world, it signals that our values, our beliefs and our culture are in support of giving everyone a fair go and bringing something to our society that can benefit us all. Australians believe in those who try hard, in those who work hard and is those who seek to benefit others.

Australia is fortunate to have been founded on institutions, beliefs and ideals established in the United Kingdom and Europe and brought to our shores with the establishment of British settlement in 1788. These early settlers brought with them the values of liberty, toleration, religious plurality and economic freedom. They also brought with them Christianity which is the intellectual and religious foundation for the centrality of the individual. The notion that you have rights, freedom and responsibilities is largely the gift of Christianity. It is also the central reasons so many others are keen to join with us in our unique life and values in Australia. The equality of all people, the equal value of men and women, the value of non-discrimination because of your race, colour, family background, class or tribe are all unique ideas given to us by Western Civilisation and Christianity. No other faith or set of ideas has given such wide benefits to individuals throughout the world and to Australia in particular.

This is the reason that all Australians have the opportunities that we do. In Australia, as Mission Engage asserts you have the opportunity and the ability to develop and form your own life, establish your own business, practice your own faith, live where you wish, develop your own friendships and bring your own life to its own fullness.

This is not the case in many parts of the world. In Islamic societies the position of women and non-Muslims is severely restricted. In Communist nations, travel rights, religious freedoms and what you can think or say is also censored and often prohibited. Mission Engage continues to encourage all those who participate in its programs to not be deterred from achieving your best. Those who have gone before us challenge us to be the best we can be, to develop our individual ideas and values and to do so for the service of others.

In short, Western civilisation and its Australian expression has given us a unique opportunity, to try new things, to develop our minds and personalities, to take charge of our economic future and to offer to others the freedom that we enjoy. Mission Engage does not tire in its encouragement to be your best as we continue to be grateful for the unique culture and values that allows us such opportunities.

- "Free speech is not just another value it's the foundation of Western Civilisation" (Jordan Peterson)

4

DON'T TALK: DO

Most human beings are great talkers, in fact I would suggest humans spend most of their time talking. Much of this is either talking about themselves or talking about what they are going to do. Action on the other hand is rare.

People seem loath to commit themselves to doing or following through on their talk. This is why getting fit is so hard for most, getting fit is always something that can be put off to another time. This is why losing weight seems beyond many people - easy to talk about much harder to actually 'do'. This is why learning a new skill or a new hobby is so difficult, easy to talk about, but also easy to talk about all the barriers to doing … I don't have the time, I don't have the money, I don't have someone to do it with …. excuses come in the millions, Action is rare.

If we are honest, we must recognise that there cannot be any achievement without action and much more seriously there cannot be a worthwhile life or a decent form of living unless there is action and doing. Action and achievement are things that comes from within, but they can be learnt and achieved by patience and practice. No one can give you anything worthwhile, you must make the decision to 'do' things for yourself.

Naturally, when we are so used to hearing about all the 'barriers' to doing, it's unusual to meet or hear of people who are not blocked by their own excuses or laziness.

Kyle Maynard is an individual so unrestricted by barriers that in 2008 he was able to climb the 19,400 feet Mount Kilimanjaro with no arms or legs. Kyle who was born with severe physical defects has long been told by others the things he cannot do. He was told he cannot live alone, he would not drive a car, he could not achieve university study and he couldn't be involved in sports. Kyle has overcome all these obstacles. When Kyle took up wrestling at University he lost his first 38 bouts but has now turned himself into a serious and respected competitor. Kyle lives by simple yet profound precepts "every excuse we make keeps us away from the things we want most in life" and "I may look disabled, but I am not!

When Kyle announced that he wanted to climb Mount Kilimanjaro his doctors said, "no way", others thought he was delusional, some were deeply critical suggesting it was all a 'Joke', but as Kyle himself noted "the world has never been tailored to my needs". Kyle's climb of Mount Kilimanjaro took weeks and included a 40 kilometre walk just to reach the mountain's base. The journey for Kyle was not easy and he contemplated giving up a number of times yet after fourteen days he reached the top of Kilimanjaro. At the peak he also revealed that he had carried the ashes of a soldier killed in Iraq, at the request of the soldier's widow. Even on this journey it had not been exclusively about Kyle. As Kyle noted at the end of the climb "the desire to do something greater in life is worth it."

Kyle Maynard lives a profound life of achievement against barriers and those keen to tell him what he cannot do, yet his life philosophy is something we can all acquire "make no excuses". Kyle Maynard is a challenge for all of us, when we are dealt a bad hand in life, do we run away or give up or do we determine to make something better of our circumstances.

Unfortunately, in modern Australia, too many of us elect to give up, too many of us act as if we are powerless, tired, stressed or just go to bed. Every day you will hear the endless complaints of others or you will hear that someone else or the government should fix the problem. We must be realistic about these 'words' and what they really mean. They are the language of people who cannot fix their own lives and will have nothing to offer you on yours.

The truth lies elsewhere and is seen in the life of Kyle Maynard and others who 'do'. It doesn't matter what happens to you in life, it doesn't matter what your background is, the great question is what you will do with what you've been given.

It is certainly true that life is not fair or easy and that sometimes the future looks bleak. But the way forward is clear, no excuses and no exception, it's your life: Don't talk do!

VITAL CHALLENGES FROM MISSION ENGAGE YOUTH

- "You can't get much done in life, if you only work on the days when you feel good" (Anonymous)

- "The vision of a champion is someone who is bent over drenched in sweat, at the point of exhaustion – when no one else is watching" (Anonymous)

- "No-one builds a legacy by standing still" (Oscar Aulig-ice)

5

WALK THROUGH THE DOOR

At Mission Engage, we have one constant message, all participates hear this over and over again: Walk through the door, take whatever is offered to you, you are not defined by your first job, the hardest step is your first. After this message we move to our second principle, ask yourself 'what next' but that's getting ahead of ourselves, the most serious and important step is to grab your first opportunity.

It never ceases to amaze me that this simple message is such a shock to people and that it is so vigorously resisted. Unfortunately, this message challenges many peoples view about themselves, there are some jobs they will not do. I am often told 'you can get me a job, but I won't to do anything where I get my hands dirty, I won't do anything that deals with the public or I won't do anything with an early start, shift work or weekend work. At this point many people are making a significant mistake, they are happy to work but they define work by what they won't do, not what work actually gives you and importantly what it leads to.

The truth of work, like life, is that we all start at the bottom and overwhelmingly those who stay at the bottom do so because they are too rigid about what the future holds and what they're worth. In every business I have ever worked the stories of the Senior Managers or the CEOs are all the same. "I started at the bottom. I learnt how to do a job that doesn't exist anymore, but I worked my way up and now I run the company". This journey of work through to the top positions may take 25-30 years but the real mistake is not being willing to take the first step.

Incredibly this mistake is usually committed by us, against ourselves with the partners in crime being our parents, families and friends. I have lost count of the number of mothers and family members who have told me that the job their son or daughter has commenced is paid too low. That the type of employment they do is tiring, or too hard to get to, or involves inconvenient early starts. Indignity at a first job from those who surround a new worker is easy but let's be truthful about what this is. This is nothing but sabotage and unfortunately a sabotage from your own family and friends who don't want to see you succeed or even do better in life than them. Regrettably then is something in many human beings that doesn't like others to succeed and the strongest expression of this hidden hostility usually comes from family and friends.

Yet, let's think about another way of seeing work. People who take these entry level jobs have a view of themselves which says, if I can just get started, if I can just jam my toe in the door, then I can get some energy and drive, then I can show people how good I am. These people have a tremendous view on work, work is the place where I make myself. Work is the vehicle that shows others who I am. Work is where I can take risks, make improvements and live life to the full. When a person views work in this way, they bring enormous benefits to a company, because they have demonstrated their intentions to better themselves and in bettering themselves they better the companies they work for.

Nevertheless, I am a realist and I know that most beginning workers don't think this way, so at Mission Engage we give lots of tips on how to do 'work and life' in a different way.

Firstly, be aware of those who talk to you in negative terms, don't just accept their advice but actively question it, what is someone really saying when they tell me I have no experience? What are they really saying when they tell me this job is disrupting my personal life? and what are they really saying when they note you don't get paid much? Almost always these negative voices come from people who don't do much themselves, who haven't advanced in their own careers or who live lives without much energy or risk.

Inertia and doing nothing is the 'living zone' for many Australians but one thing I will say without fear of contradiction, these people are not bringing much to the table of life. They do nothing new, they don't try hard things and they don't build our society for wider benefit.

We talk a lot about Australian resilience and having a go, the truth is we are mostly surrounded by people who are comfortable with what they have, even if its not much. They don't look to take action, to develop new skills or to challenge society by doing something about wrongheaded ideas.

In your working life, when you walk through the door, you

are saying something radically different about yourself. Perhaps conditions are not exactly suited to your desires and hopes but you have decided to change this, you have decided to create yourself, right now by getting up and getting moving. With these views and attitudes you become a valuable person.

- "Opportunity is missed by most people because it is dressed in overalls and looks like work (Thomas Edison)
- "The beginning is the most important part of the work" (Plato)
- "I do not know anyone who has got to the top without hard work. That is the recipe" (Margaret Thatcher)

6

CARE LESS TO SUCCEED

We have all witnessed the sports star, who under the pressure of an important game or final, with victory within their grasp seems to emotionally unravel and crash out in spectacular fashion. This might be the tennis star, who is totally overcome by a bad line call or argument with the umpire, only to see their technique and match performance evaporate. Or the golfer required to sink a putt to win a championship who freezes and misses the hole by meters. Or a footballer who has an opportunity to kick a winning goal only to blast the ball way off line for no result. The irony of all these outcomes is that in essence these are simple and repeatable skills that all these great players have performed day in, day out for many years but under the 'championship' moment something changes, and a terrible and unsuccessful result occurs.

Undoubtably, the mental stress, anxiety, panic or worry, whatever you wish to call it, has intensified within the thought process of our sports star only to see a result ending in failure. In some way, psychologically wanting something to an even greater extent has caused the complete breakdown of technique, concentration and self-confidence.

This happens to people in all kind of ways and it happens in the world of work as well. The more we convince ourselves that we urgently need this 'ideal' job, we often find that the interview process was one where we were unable to give our best.

At Mission Engage, we believe that this fear and doubt can be overcome, training helps but if training was the exclusive answer our sports stars would never fail. Something deeper is at play, what we call at Mission Engage the 'courage to not care'. This does not mean that we don't care about the outcome, or we don't care about the result, just that we see ourselves as courageous and competent individuals whatever the result, the outcome is not central, the 'doing', the process or getting the techniques correct is where our emphasis and concentration should rest. We can see many examples from the animal world, where small and fragile animals have attacked and defeated much larger predators, defeating and terrorising, an adversary who enjoys significant physical and fighting advantage. I have seen domestic cats attack marauding bears, squirrels attack venomous snakes and small dogs attack unknown humans. Usually, this is the result of a 'territory' drive in that this animal is defending its patch, or its young from a known predator. Yet, it is significant that the skills or fighting competence of the small creature doesn't seem to be relevant. What drives its success in the willingness to enter the fight and the courage to complete the ordeal whatever the cost. Almost always this 'courage and commitment' results in a surprising victory.

Humans who are looking for work, can be the same, but it is

no good practicing or preparing for what you already know, what is central is to develop your 'courage' in the face of things you don't know and can't foretell. Ironically, freedom from fear and disturbance in human life comes from constantly expecting it, we cannot predict what will come at us, but we can focus on solving new problems and not reacting to them or freezing in their wake.

Very little of what we undertake in the Australia has the potential to harm us or end our lives. A job interview does not have this potential. Small animals who successfully overcome predators are familiar with an outcome that might result in their death, but they also know they cannot be susceptible to fear or paralysis.

At Mission Engage we seek to develop resistance to the worst that can happen, we emphasise a courage born of the idea that engaging with the worst possible outcome (not getting a job) strengthens your ability to succeed in future attempts.

One of the world's greatest teachers of Jiu Jitsu, Australian John Will bans no technique on his mat, all students must learn to cope with all possibilities of attack. In this way the 'courage to engage' is highlighted and strengthened. You do not lose if you are sore or temporarily injured. The only defeat is the failure not to engage with, the real no rules world.

- Our doubts are traitors and make us lose the good we often might win by fearing to attempt" (William Shakespeare)
- What would life be if we had not courage to attempt anything" (Vincent Van Gogh)

7

FREEDOM AND THE IMPORTANCE OF YOU

Mission Engage supports and promotes the importance of your individuality and the uniqueness of your life. We see your life as exceptional and something that must be nurtured and inspired, to be the best you can be. When it comes to your life and the world of work, we believe you have a great contribution to make to our society and to wider Australia. Our country is diminished if you are not able to make the best contribution that you can make. Australia needs you!

Unfortunately, in modern Australia there are many people who don't think this way and there are groups who would prefer to see your freedom squashed and controlled by government regulation, with you being told what you can and cannot do.

At Mission Engage we believe that without the freedom of the individual there is no real freedom whether that is economic, political, religious or personal freedom.

For this reason, we do not believe you are defined by your racial or cultural background. We do not judge or make assessments about you in relation to your religion, your family, your sex or your finances. We do not make judgements about you on the basis of where you live or the way you look. At Mission Engage you are not judged on any of these group identifications, we are only interested in your improvement and development as an individual. We believe your freedom and individuality is the most important gift you have.

Nevertheless, your freedom and your individuality must be fought for. This battle begins with yourself. At Mission Engage we are challenging of people who put themselves down. We are challenging of those who won't strive to be their best and we are challenging of those who expect to receive something for nothing or those who think the world owes them work because of their background, family, race or gender. Although we highlighted the importance of the individual, we do not encourage selfish individualism that places yourself above others. At Mission Engage we emphasise unashamedly individual responsibility. We do not accept passivity, laziness or inactivity in relation to your own life and nor do we support those who would seek to control or downplay the freedom and rights of others.

It is for these reasons that we concentrate on building the resilience and toughness of your own life and we do this because we believe in the importance of you. In our programs we will expect you to take risks, we will ask you to think a great deal about your life and to be prepared to fight for it. Your future depends on your willingness to try new things, to adapt to suggestions, to put yourself forward to the best of your ability. At Mission Engage we work hard to get you a job and a future, we expect you to do the same.

So be warned, at Mission Engage we hear excuses of all sorts, but we do not accept your claims to shyness, your fears of public speaking, your statements that you have no skills or no talent or your lateness. We don't reduce our standards because your parents, friends or families will ask to make 'special arrangements' for you. We do none of these things because we think your life is too important to magically believe that you will get your act together at some stage is the future. Your life is precious and Mission Engage will only ask one thing of you, TAKE CHARGE OF IT.

- "There is nothing noble in being superior to your fellow man, true nobility is being superior to your former self." (Ernest Hemingway)
- "Those who cannot change their minds cannot change anything." (George Bernard Shaw)
- "As a human your greatness lies in not being able to remake the world but in being able to remake yourself." (Mahatma Gandhi)
- "He who conquers himself is the greatest warrior." (Confucius)

8

SMALL STEPS – LASTING IMPACT

Australians are frequently encouraged to dream or set goals on a grand scale. Our school system tells all Australian students that anything is possible and that there are no barriers to what you can achieve in life. In broad terms I agree with these sentiments, yet very few people tell you how any of these dreams and goals might actually be achieved.

I get to hear the aspirations of many young Australians, I've heard of dreams of space flight, of climbing Everest, of building great wealth, of playing test cricket, or first grade football in one of any number of codes.

I've also heard of less outwardly complicated dreams that may involve weight loss, quitting smoking, learning a language or playing an instrument.

Nevertheless, for many people there is little action, initiative or progress on these dreams that consume so much conversation and discussion.

For many people, that's what the dream remains, a topic of conversation with little link to reality. It is sad to hear individuals explain their great love of animals and their dream of becoming a vet, to discover that they have no desire to return to school or that they reject or don't like study. The same applies to those who wish to be sports stars yet acknowledge that their physical fitness is poor and that they have no plans to engage in a training routine.

For most people the disconnection between the 'life goal' and the method for reaching this goal is worlds apart. Such goals have become little more than a delusion, or a fairy tale story designed to entertain others.

Deep down many people know that such a disconnection exists that's why another layer of conversation is never far behind. This conversation concerns all the reasons and excuses we have failed to begin the journey to our goal.

These will be things like 'I don't have enough time', 'the timing is not right', 'I'm waiting for someone to help me', or 'I don't have enough money.

Yet, the reality remains, many of us have just pushed our dreams and goals further into the future, to a time or place where they will never be achieved. The reality that nothing worth having is ever easy, or that some goals will require diligence or toughness becomes the sub-conscious excuse for not beginning.

At Mission Engage we encourage a system of small steps and small goals. By all means keep the big goal but let's also breakdown our goals into manageable bites Let's ensure that we identify a small step, that we do it well and that we make the step after that small as well. Big goals are great, but Everest is reached by thousands of small steps.

At the beginning of a sporting season, no coach is prepared to talk about or contemplate winning a championship. What will be a focus is the next training session, completing a drill, finishing a workout, finishing the small task placed in front of you and finishing it to the best of your ability.

When it comes to our goals, keeping a fierce concentration on the small steps is essential to not being distracted away from them. The central point of small steps is not to focus on the big future but on the small achievable stuff.

Many Australians are easily distracted from their goals and consequently rarely achieve them. This is a sad circumstance both for the individual and our society. The reality of a small step process is to acknowledge that you can commence the journey now, not worrying about an unachievable large goal but being proud of the achievements and sustained results along the way.

Just taking a small step is infinitely better than doing nothing. Just do a little, it often leads to a lot!

- "It doesn't mean the goals we have don't count, the goals do count because they cause us to go through the process and it's the process that makes us wise and happy." (Benjamin Hoff)
- "A blooming rose bush catches the eye of admirers but remember, it grew from a seed buried in dirt." (Kristin Elizabeth)
- "A successful friendship is a process, not a goal." (Joseph Rain)

9

NO FAILURE – NO GROWTH

One of the strangest ideas bedded into our society and supported by most people is that "failure is a bad thing". Many of our insults are built around the idea that people who fail are somehow less worthy than others 'you're a loser', 'this person has never achieved anything', 'this person has lots of business ideas but they all fail.'

There is no doubting that the idea of failure and the fear of repeated failure is one of the reasons that many people give up on their dreams of the future. There is also the distinct possibility that family members, parents or your friends will be quick to tell you that you're not capable of achieving your goals, that you're not strong enough or talented enough to fulfil that future. Who do you think you are? Don't forget where you came from! All of this is really code for we don't want you to succeed and we don't want you to do anything different to us.

Of course, the truth of life is that overwhelmingly the human experience is one of failure, it's one of giving up, it's one of unfulfilled and incomplete dreams. Every human life is filled with mountains of failure, yet for some people they don't seem to notice and it doesn't seem to stop them from trying again and again.

One of my greatest heroes in life had a professional life that was riddled with failure, long periods where few people believed in him and long gaps in life without any friends or any real supporters. Winston Churchill's decisions during World War I saw him dismissed from his cabinet position, excluded from the war council and allowed no further influence in government administration. In fact, his rejection was so severe, he himself felt the only way to redeem himself was to go back to active service in the front line. He re-joined his unit in 1915 at the age of 41.

Nevertheless, this brave and humble responses to his failures still was unable to change people's opinions for another 30 years until the British people again turned to a resilient and determined Churchill as their only option to oppose an all-conquering Adolf Hitler.

Winston Churchill was not made of a different substance than you and I. He was not a superman and nor was he a man who was unaware of his many failures. But he was able to keep going, to change course, to improve and to do 'life' differently. Why? What was the one thing that gave Churchill such an apparent resilience in the face of endless obstacles and disappointments.

In my view, Churchill had subconsciously made an important connection: failure and action are intimately connected. This is a connection that is not often made because, overwhelmingly when people fail they stop acting. For a majority of us, failure means stopping, when most people fall off a horse they don't get back on, the pain of failure, the embarrassment, the fact that others note your failure – all contribute to the majority of us giving up.

For an individual like Churchill, failure meant more action, not less, failure meant questions about how things can be done differently, and failure meant new ways of 'doing' or approaching the tasks. What if we could consider failure as the gateway to a new way of 'doing things'? What if failure could be seen as the necessary first step towards the onset of breakthroughs and success? What if we were no longer embarrassed by failure but stimulated by it as the path to great success.

Last year I heard a great story of achievement. This story involves a young man with physical and psychological disabilities who took up martial arts. On his first lesson, he could not manage a warm-up star jump, he could not master a forward roll, he could not speak to strangers and he could not understand basic instructions. Nevertheless, this man attended class faithfully 4 nights a week, catching long bus trips to and from training. For years and years his nightly experience was one of failure and starting again. No one in his school made it easy for him. In 2018 after 13 years of training he finally achieved his black belt and made a heartfelt and intelligent acceptance speech in a public forum. Is this young man the best black belt in his school, no he is not, but is this one of the greatest achievements in Australian sport, yes, it is! Of course, there are millions of better sports people whose skills and performance are widely admired. Given the starting point of this young man there are few greater individual achievements against adversity and failure.

I doubt many of us would be able to persevere in this way, yet again there is in this story a strong connection between failure and action. Within this failure and the slowness of learning, is still the foundation of a willingness to learn, to try another approach, to listen, and start again.

In continuous failure both Churchill and this young martial artist learnt that exposure to challenging circumstances made them mentally stronger. Small failures over and over inoculate them against disappointment. Ultimately, it was not failure that showed these men success but their response that made that possible.

- "Failure is simply the opportunity to begin again, this time more intelligently." (Henry Ford)
- "Success is not final, failure is not fatal: it is the courage to continue that counts." (Winston Churchill)
- "Our greatest weakness lies in giving up. The most certain way to success is always to try just one more time." (Thomas Edison)

10

FIND THE GAP

Over the years I have interviewed many people intensely eager to acquire a job or to work for a particular company.

These applicants will usually have promoted themselves vigorously as self-starters, highly motivated with a strong desire to bring their substantial gifts and talents into your workplace. All this is notable and an admirable place to begin. Yet, it is only a beginning and there is an important aspect of their capacity which has not been highlighted.

At this point, many applicants make a significant change of direction. They begin a discussion around benefits that will accrue to them. Some will request air conditioned and spacious offices, others will insist on certain times of a year to be available for holidays, or child minding. Still others will question how often bonus and salary increases will occur.

Whilst these questions are reasonable, there is another important subject that has not been addressed. Certainly, it is essential that an individual can perform the tasks in the job description but much more valuable to an enterprising company is the ability to find the gaps, to discover what's missing in a company and to have some insight into how to develop or enhance this niche.

This ability to see and develop a new opening for a company is the beginning of creativity. This is the place where new directions and new thinking becomes possible. A person who wishes to join a company with the ability to see what might be possible is valuable beyond measure. Lots of people can do a particular job. Few are able to see how it can be done better or how it can be extended into a new avenue.

Many companies will even accept people who are shy, not confident or doubt their own abilities because the key components to creative and long-lasting work is intuition and a focus on the future.

Often people who are seeking work tell me that they cannot think this way. They insist that their strengths are found in routine, loyalty and the ability to perform a task on time and on budget. Yes, these are valuable and respected traits, but they are also shared by many of your competitors, especially the new kid on the block: The Robot!

Your perception may be that you are not inciteful and that you are not innovative. My definition of being human includes both these things. At Mission Engage we do recognise that self-doubt is real and that some individuals may never fully overcome negative images or thoughts about themselves.

Nevertheless, we also recognise that pushing yourself to achieve, adapt, change and to never give up, whilst not easy, is achievable for all who seek to claim and change their own future.

Our perceptions and our realities do not control out future. We are sometimes understood to be a difficult and pushy organisation. Yes, we are, as we have already discovered many people who once didn't believe in their ability to succeed but finally did.

We believe personal contentment is found is those who make something where there was nothing before. The comment that something 'can't be done' is not an excuse to recede into a space where all things answer to security and predictability. Our best ideas come from what has never been tried before. Don't be afraid of the gap, find it!

- "All our dreams can come true, if we have the courage to pursue them." (Walt Disney)
- "I have not failed, I just found 10,000 ways that won't work." (Thomas Edison)
- "Do, or do not. There is no try." (Yoda)
- "I've missed over 9000 shots in my career, I've lost almost 300 games. 26 times I've been trusted to take the winning shot and missed. I've failed over and over. That's why I succeed." (Michael Jordan)

11

THERE IS NO SUCH THINGS AS GENIUS- JUST BLOODY HARD WORK

We live in a world that loves talent. We hear this word use in all sorts of contexts and situations. We have talented sportspeople, talented actors and musicians, talented politicians, we even have talented newsreaders and TV hosts!

Whilst we are always talking about looking for new talent, developing talent, channelling talent, the truth is that very few people have natural born expertise or aptitude. What we do have is capacity and room for improvement, but no one has an innate ability that will take them to the top without effort.

Indeed, our infatuation with discovering talent often means we crush the interest and passion of young people by driving them to achieve or perform against their natural desires. We can see this most clearly in parents who drive their children to succeed in sports or academic subjects where the child's interests are not found.

The world is full of allegedly talented people who end up doing nothing with their lives, achieving nothing and contributing nothing. Labelling people as 'talented' is a significant curse on obtaining success, as relying on talent alone is a dead end.

True success lies in other areas. Persistence and determination!

Successful people display two characteristics that can be copied by all of us: A strong work ethic and a never give up attitude. This is easy to say but far from easy to do.

It is true that most humans, give up easily, stop trying when obstacles are placed in our way and revert to a defeatism that suggests life is 'unfair'. Success never accepts the action of giving up or accepting that a goal cannot to obtained.

It is often argued that Winston Churchill was the greatest person of the twentieth century. I am very happy to agree with this statement yet if we are to look at his life seriously we must conclude that his life was also heavily marked by failure, insolation, loneliness and hostility. Most things in life that Churchill undertook ended in failure.

Both his parents were distant to him and without real affection, he was a poor student, spending all of his primary years in the bottom class. He failed his entrance to Harrow School but was likely admitted through his family's payment of extra fees.

At 18 Churchill joined the Army but again failure entrance examinations for the Regiments of his choice.

On his eighteen birthday his father wrote the following lines, "Because I am certain that if you cannot prevent yourself from leading the idle and useless life you have had through your schoolings, you will degenerate into a shabby, unhappy and futile existence. If that is so you will bear all the blame yourself".

Churchill was always in a poor physical state and experienced chest infections, depression and hives all throughout his life.

His early political career was marked by the disaster of Gallipoli, (which he was blamed for) and the rejection both of voters and friends. After 25 years in the political wilderness Churchill was finally called upon to be British Prime Minister during World War II. Churchill's determination and resilience won him this job, which he used to steel England against invasion and to ultimately win World War II.

His reward for this profound leadership was to be defeated at the first election after the wars end! Churchill's success during World War II was never founded on popularity but on holding onto views he considered to be the truth and living them regardless of the personal consequences. These are the things that make a great person.

Abraham Lincoln was the sixteenth president of the United States, guiding the country through the American Civil War, perhaps its greatest moral and political crisis. Nevertheless, Lincoln had a similar life to Churchill and his life and career was marked by extreme failure.

He was born into poverty. He failed in business twice and was declared bankrupt. He suffered a nervous breakdown and endured the death of his fiancé just weeks before their marriage. In 1832 Lincoln lost his job, tried to go to law school but couldn't get in. In 1833, he borrowed some money to begin a business which failed and spent the next 17 years paying off his debt.

Finally, after eight election losses, in 1860 Lincoln was elected president of the United States. Lincoln is often held up as the great example that anyone can make it in the United States. What is not told in Lincoln's life story is the long years of isolation and defeat and his profound ability to continue to work hard, start again, try new approaches and most importantly to never give up.

Both Churchill and Lincoln believed in values they were not prepared to compromise. Both promoted freedom and liberty and ultimately were prepared to fight for their beliefs. Despite regular defeats they both believed the more you put into your life, the more you receive. They were also not prepared to comprise the things that nobody can take from you – your integrity, your honesty and your authenticity.

At Mission Engage we know that defeats, knockbacks, failures and disappointments make up a great deal of life. Yet, we also know that personal integrity, honest determination and hard work do get results. As Churchill and Lincoln both show it's not over when your failing terribly…its only over when you quit.

- "Continuous effort, not strength or intelligence is the key to unlocking your potential." (Winston Churchill)
- "You have enemies? Good, that means you stood up for something in your life." (Winston Churchill)

- "Never give in, never give in, never, never, never, never – in nothing great or small, large or petty – never give in except to convictions of honour and good." (Winston Churchill)
- "Anyone who has never failed has never tried anything new." (Albert Einstein)
- "It's not that I'm smart – I just stay with problems longer." (Albert Einstein)
- "You never fail until you stop trying." (Albert Einstein
- "My great concern is not whether you have failed, but whether you are content with your failure." (Abraham Lincoln)
- "You cannot help men by doing for them what they could and should do for themselves." (Abraham Lincoln)

12

CREATING AND SUSTAINING ENERGY

Perhaps the greatest set of complaints people make about their lives centre around lack of energy. This is often packaged as tiredness, lack of motivation, an inability to sleep, or just a more basic, I can't be bothered, or it's not worth the effort.

Lack of energy is a huge blockage to engagement with the world and ultimately making and sustaining a purposeful life. What is often unconsidered or unknown to people who talk regularly about their lack of motivation and energy is that it is possibly the greatest barrier to making new friends, finding work or contributing to our world.

After all, who wants to surround themselves with people who constantly need motivation and encouragement to act? A person who regularly uses the language of 'no energy' will quickly become someone who is not invited to events, not offered work opportunities and not considered for demanding or interesting roles.

The person of no energy sabotages and undermines their own life. Most people subconsciously do not want to associate with or employ those who drain energy from others with demotivating language and lack of action.

If I need to motivate you to go to a game of football with me then eventually I will stop asking you. When we are looking for a job, or developing a career, knockbacks, rejections or no replies to applications is a common event. It happens to all of us and is not specific to only one field of endeavour. Yet for many it becomes overwhelming and contributes to lack of energy or just giving up.

Dealing with frequent rejection is an unpleasant and harsh experience, yet there is a positive and successful method to managing these difficult moments. This involves layering your life to include more touchpoints with people and activities.

The key point of this idea is that the more layers, interests and activities, the more energy you will have. Invariably, people who lack energy and motivation have narrowed their lives to the point where not much actually happens. A diet of home or television or internet will lead eventually to a shortage of friendships, job opportunities and diverse groups with which to interact.

Sustaining energy is intimately linked to having your fingers in many pies, joining sporting clubs, taking up hobbies, or volunteering for community groups. This does two powerful things. It links you to new people and it allows you to experience different ways of thinking.

I have met people who have never actually been for a job interview, all their work opportunities come through the friends and acquaintances, they have met through the activities they pursue. People in clubs notice your volunteerism, they notice your desire to help and improve the club and they notice your positive attitudes.

Placing yourself is such positions gives you a huge advantage over strangers and those only able to attract attention through internet applications. The human network is still the best mechanism for finding work opportunities but more importantly the best mechanism for developing friendships and improving yourself.

Some of the most interesting research coming out of World War II concerned those who were imprisoned or within camps for considerable periods of time. Significantly, those who lived longer, stayed healthier and were not prone to suicide, were those who attacked each day in a positive manner, shaving, washing, cleaning clothes, talking with and learning new hobbies from others dramatically increased survival rates.

On the other hand, those who became isolated couldn't be bothered to talk, lay on their beds and complained of illness, tiredness or hopeless thoughts, often did not survive the experience of long captivity

The good news for us in modern Australia is the wonderful number of opportunities for new experiences that we all have. Taking these possibilities is the key to sustaining personal energy.

- "Every great and commanding movement in the world is due to the triumph of personal energy." (Ralph Waldo Emerson)

- "We act as though comfort and luxury were the chief requirements of life, yet what really makes us happy is something to be enthusiastic about." (C. Kingsley)

- "The most powerful weapon on earth is the human soul on fire." (General Ferdinand Foch)

- "Energy and persistence conquer all things." (Benjamin Franklin)

13

CULTIVATING EXCELLENCE

Australian society is full of city buildings, houses, products and consumer goods that are functional, yet inexpensive and designed not to last. Indeed, much of this is little more than rubbish that will be sent to our garbage dumps within a year or two.

It's also the case that many of our roads, infrastructure, cars, sporting goods, phones, televisions and clothing is of poor quality, made quickly and with faults that already exist at the time of purchase. The world we live in sees very little that is built to last or indeed is designed to be available to anyone beyond the initial purchaser.

In a world where material goods are so poorly made and have little value why would anyone recommend that young Australians strive for excellence or strive to provide lasting impact on the lives of those whom we meet? What's the point and relevance of excellence in a world that suggests most things will be discarded in a few short years?

Most Australians only visit Cathedrals and Ancient buildings on our travels to Europe. Indeed many don't go into these buildings even as tourists. Those who do discover something that is hard to find in general life. They find and experience a sense of awe!

The wonder and amazement found in these Ancient buildings prompts a lot of questions. Why did people wish to construct such structures? What are they saying about life? and why did they put such veneration and reverence into even the smallest parts of their construction?

Essentially, these buildings were designed to lift the human spirit and soul towards God, towards a beauty and depth that we rarely see in this life. Yet they also tell us something central about humanity. We are creatures designed to replicate the skills and beauty found in creation, and we reach our greatest fulfilment when we strive to live lives of beauty and excellence.

This is one of the reasons I get so frustrated when Christians who say they believe in awe, wonder and beauty fail to construct classic, permanent and beautiful buildings, yes you can worship God in a tin shed but that is not what we humans are called to be, we are called to be people of excellence and beauty, something beyond ourselves, something that speaks of our care, concern and love for others.

Australian life also sees a lack of excellence in the services that we call upon to sustain and improve our lives. This is seen in the poor quality of government and private providers. Many of our train, trams and buses are old, dirty and don't run on time. Our streets are uncleaned, rubbish collections are poor. Internet services are weak, medical, dental and optical facilities are no longer cutting edge.

We live in a world where the demand of services is often unfilled, maintenance providers are hard to find and those who do manage to be available are overworked and provide only temporary fixes. Short term functionality and inexpensive outcomes seem to have infected the thinking and expectations on those who provide much needed services into our lives. This lack of excellence and attention to detail is also seen in our personal lives.

Recently, Victoria has seen a dramatic increase in both the purchase of boats but also an increase in drowning deaths at sea. Whilst more safety equipment is provided into modern watercraft, the owners remain totally unfamiliar with their operation. 40% of deaths from drowning are of people on boats who are unable to swim and have consumed alcohol levels between 2 and 4 times those required to safely handle a car, yet no consideration was given to the risks of boat operation and safety equipment whilst full of alcohol.

A lack of excellence in such personal requirements admits to the idea that poor standard and poor personal performance are okay and acceptable even with our own lives and the lives of others.

Mission Engage always empathises striving for excellence and that excellence is an important value that comes from within. If you cannot perform at your best, even when no one is watching, then how can you convince others that value is part of who you are. If your home or personal space is dirty, messy and uncleaned then how can you convince others your work performance will be of a high standard.

I make this point regularly to taxi drivers. If your car is dirty, then why should I assume you know how to get me to my destination safely and efficiently. I'm sad to say I am always proved right on this point and others agree too. Uber largely owes is success to this situation.

At Mission Engage we emphasise excellence by challenging people to take the hard road. It is in conquering the hard and difficult aspects of a task that brings excellence to the easier parts.

In my own life I experienced this recently. Learning to hover a helicopter is a difficult task and a task not easily taught. Each student must overcome the complications in their own way. Yet surprisingly the task of hovering in higher winds which is much harder, results in a better and smoother hover in low winds. When we aim to achieve the difficult aspects of life we find the more mundane tasks obtainable in easier fashion.

Yet it is the driving of excellence in the difficult moments that drives excellence in the easier parts. Always be wary of those who put off and make excuses in performing relatively simple tasks, they will invariably be found missing when the going is tough. Excellence is born not from just doing enough, but from mastering the complex.

Another important component of excellence is watching and studying the behaviours of the best. Any reasonable coach can teach you a forehand tennis shot but learning and studying from the best shows you how to train, where to apply the shot, how to set up in a match and how to make such a shot work in difficult circumstances.

Again, choosing a more difficult or longer path result in learning that is deeper and more widely applicable. Excellence is not found in short cuts but taking the long way to understanding. Finally, excellence is driven by things that most people overlook. When you say yes you will do something, do what you say. Excellence is found is completing tasks efficiently and without fuss. When you are able to complete tasks well and in a timely way, you indicate to others that you are a trustworthy person and that your words and speech mean something.

Australia is full of people who are great talkers and who make lots of promises about performing jobs but never seem to achieve them. If you rely on such individuals you are likely to be disappointed. I always choose people who do what they say, this reliability is the bedrock of a person who values and lives by excellence and personal honour.

- "We are what we repeatedly do. Excellence is not an act but a habit." (Aristotle)
- "If you are going to achieve excellence in big things, you develop the habit in little matters." (General Colin Powell)

- "The quality of a person's life is in direct proportion to their commitment to excellence." (Vince Lombardi)
- "The noblest search is the search for excellence." (President Lyndon B Johnston)
- "He who is faithful in little will be faithful in much." (Jesus Christ)

14

BLACK HOLES: DRUGS, ALCOHOL AND CRIME

A life, a career, a family or a future can be derailed by any number of circumstances. Many have their origin in the unpredictability of life. Nevertheless, there are three that are particularly ruthless and unrelenting and are always linked to human free will. Drugs, Alcohol and Crime are entirely affected by human choice. Undertaken and sustained by choice and ultimately only fixed by choice.

In modern Australia, which always seeks reasons for disaster beyond the individual, Mission Engage has a particularly strong and stark message: The choice to take drugs, drink alcohol or become involved in crime rests with individual choice. It amounts to a stupid and unintelligent choice and is guaranteed to impede and prevent your life coming to its fullness.

Those who undertake such activities risk frustrating their own hopes and dreams and sacrificing their lives in a garbage dump of nothingness. These three black holes are acutely severe because they always result in either a long journey of recovery or no recovery at all. They are fundamentally a destroyer of lives for those who are unaware of their destructive power or those who choose to treat them frivolously.

At Mission Engage we see no moral case for accepting these choices as genuine ways of fulfilling your life. Mission Engage sees undertaking any of these choices as little more than giving up on effort, self-improvement and responsibility to yourself. At Mission Engage we proudly see hard work and steady improvement as the source of human fulfilment. The black holes of Drugs, Alcohol and Crime are little more than self-deception and delusion.

Overwhelmingly, the effect of prolonged drug or alcohol abuse result in a debilitating transformation of life. Motivation and interests in your life's plans and goals become harder to sustain and in most cases, they disappear. Passions for achievements and the desire to learn new skills also crumble. Those living within these black holes become content with not changing. Expectations, enthusiasm and love of life are drained and apathy, laziness and a desire to do nothing takes over. The opportunities of work or career changes are passed over.

The desire to be left alone, doing your own thing becomes stronger and the likelihood of disconnection from family and friends becomes greater. Those involved in Drugs, Alcohol and Crime are isolated, increasingly without friends and only concerned with the immediate problem of finding the next source of short-term pleasure. The ability or inclination to work consistently is trashed, which results in an inability to save money, build wealth or plan for a worthwhile future. Those involved in these black holes are unhappy and subject to changes in mental health.

Cocaine is noted for its strong connection to strokes, brain haemorrhages, heart attacks, convulsions and delirium. Heroin is known to decrease life expectancy and contains a high risk of serious infection through shared needles. Those is this position are unable to undertake work, living conditions get worse and the possibility of a happy life disappears fast.

It is also important to note that treatment for the 'black holes' is long, arduous and almost always fails in the first few attempts. All successful treatment programs rely heavily on the participants will power and desire to change their lives. If this is not present and the individual does not want to stop, then no improvement is possible.

At Mission Engage we focus on developing the strength of an individual's character and purpose so that the "black holes" can be clearly seen as the dead ends they are. We consider that we are all responsible for our own lives and actions and that dulling our senses is a useless and ineffective way of dealing with the discontent of life. If the world is at fault or we are at fault, we seek to change the world and ourselves for the better, withdrawing from the world solves nothing.

- "Drug use begins with the hope that something 'out there' can instantly fill up the emptiness inside." (Jean Kilbourne)
- "Drug misuse is not a disease, it's a decision – like the decision to step out in front of a moving car." (Phillip K. Dick)
- "Drugs are a waste of time, they destroy your memory and your self-respect and everything that goes along with your self-esteem." (Kurt Cobain)

- "The experiment which drugs induce are as far removed from reality as is a mirage, from water. No matter how much you pursue the mirage, you will never quench your thirst." (Meher Baba)

- Macbeth "Canst them not minister to a mind diseased, raise out the written troubles of the brain, cleanse the bosom of that which weighs upon the heart?"

- Physician "Therein the patient must minister to himself." (William Shakespeare)

15

DEAD END THINKING

Human living guarantees that at some stage in our lives we will be hurt by others. Perhaps our parents have hurt us through their actions or lack of care over a number of years. Perhaps they have been absent from our lives or abandoned us in our early years. Most of us will have been hurt during relationships, feeling that a former partner, friend or lover was dishonest or unfaithful towards us.

All humans will have periods in life where friends or work colleagues let us down and are false hearted in their actions. These moments can cause us to often have thoughts and comments about others that perhaps we don't really mean but can quickly get established in our thinking suggesting that our experience somehow reflects a truth about all 'types' of certain people.

Of course, it's easy for a woman after a break up with a man to suggest this is typical male behaviour. 'All men are bastards' is usually just a silly throwaway line but for some people such thinking becomes imbedded as a truth and as a narrative on which to guide all future relationships with men. A person who buys into such a shallow story about other types of people commonly goes on to ensure a life of little trust becomes the norm in their future encounters with others. A pattern established on this shallow thinking can be hard to change. Once we begin to see this pattern applying to all people its usually possible to easily 'create' the 'truth' to back such assertions.

In the same way men who consider that all women cannot be trusted or have tendencies to gossip are applying a poorly thought out logic to 50% of the population. Such thinking is unproductive on many levels as it blinds us to the very same characteristics in groups we think don't behave this way or in ourselves. Individuals who think that gossip is a female characteristic haven't listened to a talk back radio or football shows or have forgotten their own constant chatter on who could be 'traded' or 'delisted' by their own team in future seasons.

Dead end thinking can be heard in many conversations, but it is most commonly packaged in discontented or annoyed formats. Being aware of these irritated discussions can help safeguard our own thinking or at least help us acknowledge the lack of logic or clarity in many discussions.

Individuals who feel that they are owed something by a workplace or that a government should be doing more to fix problems or that their race, background or culture gives them special insights are often sinking into dead end thinking. This thinking always suggests that 'others', those outside of myself are responsible for my disaster or lack of progress.

Unfortunately, significant numbers of people have developed this stilted form of thinking. This inevitably causes problems and conflicts in personal and work life but more importantly blocks and prevents the personal maturity we need to flourish in life.

At Mission Engage we suggest that freedom and personal growth come from within. Your personal viewpoints are not our business, but we do suggest that all Australians of whatever background or culture can make a positive contribution to our society. For Mission Engage, what really counts is that you live by your own achievements and your own effects.

- "Parents can only give good advice or put them on the right path, but the final forming of a person's character lies in their own hands." (Anne Frank)
- "There is an expiry date for blaming your parents, for steering you in the wrong direction; the moment you are old enough to take the wheel, responsibility lies with you." (J.K Rowling)
- "Attack the evil that is within yourself, rather than attacking the evil that is in others." (Confucius)
- "The victim's mindset destroys human potential. By not accepting personal responsibility for our circumstances, we greatly reduce our power to change them." (Steve Maraboli)
- "When others bewail the failure of government, you must speak of self-reliance, of personal responsibility, of individual pride and integrity. When others preach

compromise, you must preach conviction." (Margaret Thatcher)

- "There is no such thing as entitlement unless someone has first met an obligation." (Margaret Thatcher)
- "To those whom much is given much is expected." (Jesus Christ)

16

THE TRICKY GOD QUESTION

Prior to considering any of the tricky questions surrounding God, we need an honest appraisal of the way modern Australia actually is. Unquestionably, younger Australians are under great stress and enticement in regard to social issues. The impact of drugs, mental health, alcohol, depression, anxiety, family breakdown, unemployment and crime have resulted in increasing numbers of young Australians finding it hard to integrate into society and make a meaningful contribution to it.

Young Australians have higher rates in depression and seek medical and psychological treatment at levels not seen previously in our national history. This state of affairs is not new and has been unfolding for perhaps the last 25-30 years. It does appear that neither our educational or medical experts have answers that are viable or effective.

At Mission Engage we believe that the individual is in control of his or her life and can through determination and application shape life to be a successful and profound experience both for themselves and their society. Nevertheless, there are a number of important questions that must be asked of ourselves if we are to shape our lives in beneficial ways. These are all internal questions that must be answered by each individual, in their own way and cannot be avoided or passed to others. Why am I here? What is the purpose of my life? What is the meaning of life? What am I meant to do with my life?

The truth of Australian society is that these questions are not fully considered or that the answers given only contain partial truth. Certainly, it is possible to mask internal emptiness through many of the solutions we employ, but the questions remain, only the symptoms are partially blocked. Clearly, drugs, alcohol or anti-depressants can distract or temporarily make individuals feel secure and comfortable. But, the impact is short lived, the questions remain and the costs to our bodies and souls is often damaging.

In my profession I deal with a substantial number of people who are considering suicide. In my view no individual considers such an act when the 'why' questions of life have been answered effectively. In the same way, continued drug or alcohol use always has at its base unanswered questions about, who am I? and what is the meaning of my life?

Mission Engage is not a religious organisation and is not involved in any forms of evangelisation, our purpose is to prepare and encourage young Australians to enter the workforce. We believe the dignity of work is essential for all young Australians.

Nevertheless, we also know that many young Australians self-sabotage possibilities of an effective work life by distractions that are unhelpful. People who are unsure of who they are mostly find demands of work a considerable burden. Therefore, we do subscribe to the famous maxim of St Augustine 'Our hearts are restless until they rest in God.' Why am I here? And what is my purpose in life? may not for all people have a foundation in God but it is still a question that requires an answer.

- "The mystery of human existence lies not just is staying alive but in finding something to live for." (Fydor Dostoyevski)
- "If a man hasn't discovered something he will die for he isn't fit to live." (Martin Luther King Jr)
- "The reason most people suffer is not that life is too tough, its that they haven't found anything worth living for." (Alexander Den Heijer)
- "Our hearts are restless until they rest in God." (St Augustine)

17

KITCHEN SINK TO MICHELIN CHEF

In recent years Australian television has become saturated with reality, competitive cooking shows. These programs have become massively popular. Featuring famous local chefs and food critics as judges along with competitive participants, striving for substantial prizes.

An outcome of this expose has been a dramatic increase in the number of Australians who consider themselves skilled in food preparation and presentation. What is generally overlooked is the huge discrepancy between arm chair competence and the long, hot, stressful hours that most chefs undertake, often for many years and with little financial reward.

I have had the wonderful privilege of implementing our Mission Engage program with Crown Chief Executive Chef Stephane Le Grand. He tells an inspiring story of his early years, compelled by his father as a twelve-year-old to begin work in a local restaurant as a dishwasher. His father's view that he would not amount to much has been proven totally wrong as Stephane became captivated by the skills, diligence and work ethic of a small local French restaurant. Stephane's enthusiasm, determination and a constant desire to ask questions and try new things has seen him rise to the very top of his profession.

Nevertheless, as he tells Mission Engage participants you should be aware of the truth; you will go through long hours, hard times and fluctuating financial and business outcomes. The journey to be a professional chef is littered with ups and downs and many who start out on the journey will fall by the wayside. Stephane's message is very clear and profound, if you really desire to be a chef, you must start at the bottom and like him you must begin at the kitchen sink.

This message is not what most people want to hear and unfortunately not what most are prepared to do. In each of our courses Stephane has offered work to our participants in some of Melbourne's best restaurants but always at the kitchen sink. In our many courses to date no one has embraced this opportunity.

Sometimes, on the road to where we want to go we have to do things we would rather not do. Perhaps the vision of most people does not envisage a professional well-paid career beginning at the boring, dirty grind of dishwashing. But it does and according to Stephane it goes much deeper.

Many people who have dropped out of expensive and demanding culinary courses have asked Stephane, where they went wrong and how to ensure success in a future try. He only recommends one thing – go back to the dishes. Do six months there and learn to love this craft. Many people tell Stephane that this advice has changed their life and approach to culinary skills and performance. When we can love the grubby how much more can we understand and value the beauty?

There is nothing shameful about beginning at the kitchen sink, it is the place and first opportunity to excel and to learn excellence. To all people who turn their backs on tasks they think are beneath them, a key learning is lost. Everything we do matters, and every job is a chance to be your best. Wherever we are and whatever we are doing we owe it to ourselves to be our best. Learn this and you will always see the dignity and beauty in all work.

It is hard to add to these profound thoughts of Stephane Le Grand, I would only suggest one other significant dimension to work. Yes, it is important to be paid for the work you do, as Jesus himself said "The labourer is worthy of his hire" but there is another layer to the dignity of work and that is when you are prepared to work for someone who cannot pay you or who cannot notice you. When you do something for others for free, you really begin to understand the importance of work for all of us. In working for someone who cannot see you or thank you, you truly acknowledged the beauty, inspiration and power that work can give. In doing such actions we have moved beyond duty and rights into mastery and creativity. How you do anything is how you will do everything.

- "No work is insignificant. All labour that uplifts humanity has dignity." (Martin Luther King Jr)

- "We work to become, not to acquire." (Elbert Hubbard)
- "No man was ever glorious, who was not laborious." (Benjamin Franklin)
- "To labour is to pray." (Rule of St Benedict)

18

SEIZING ADVERSITY

Hard times, troubles, adversity, bad luck and sickness happen to every human being on the planet. It is one of our common experiences as humans. You might not know anything about another person's life but one thing you can be sure of is that they carry some form of suffering and adversity in their lives.

Given how common human disasters and misfortune is, you might expect us to be a little more prepared for its arrival and be a little more honest in the ways we deal with it. But, no, overwhelmingly most humans never consider its arrival in their lives and are mostly unskilled in dealing with its consequences. Hence, the advent of tough times usually freezes us in the headlights, causes us psychological upset, brings out anger, frustration and hostility in some and causes a few to question the whole purpose of life.

Yet, what if it didn't have to be like this? What if we could mostly see our lives in big picture format. What if we were constantly looking not only to what is immediately in front of us but what are the larger opportunities to fulfil our goals and live a bit more authentically?

People often talk about changing their lives, most seem unable to do it. I would like to suggest two positive ways you might make real change. The first one is to get used to adversity. The best way to do this is to get more of it in your life. The more you wrestle with adversity and defeat it, the stronger we become and the less are its affects upon us.

This always means not taking short cuts in life but being prepared to sit and wait upon a problem, to study it, to understand its affects, in short to get into the mud and embrace all of its dimensions. It may be that we have been abandoned by a partner or a lover, this person may have seemed the only one for you.... but was that really the truth?

Was there everything about this person, their family, their work and their values really so perfect? Were their little moments when you yourself may have felt compromised in their presence? Did they allow you sufficient freedom and the ability to be yourself? Were you always the one who paid? A deep analysis, really opening yourself to the full dimensions of this relationship does not come without pain, but then you may find that the changes demanded in your life could not have been sustained.

In love and wider life, we often live by stereotypes, loving a complex and less than perfect person is a whole other matter. Only such wrestling can help us to be stronger in the future. To build resilience and character and not to fall in love with another person who turns out to be similar in personality and nature. Seizing the pain and learning gives life a whole new perspective and importantly a whole new depth.

Another option is to live more deeply for the things you believe in. Strengthen them and you find that the tough times are often more about our own fears than about the outside forces. I find Max Kolbe to be perhaps the most powerful saint of the twentieth century. A Catholic priest who opposed the Nazis in World War II, he was finally arrested for operating an underground newspaper and sent to Auschwitz.

During his time any escaping prisoners saw other prisoners 'decimated' (an ancient Roman practice of killing 10 for each one who had escaped) Kolbe was not one of the few selected to be killed but when he heard another prisoner begging for his life, he stepped forward to exchange with him. This offer was accepted. It took 3 weeks for Kolbe to be starved to death, during which time his guards needed to be changed every few hours. His joy in sharing the life of Jesus was apparently converting too many guards! Max Kolbe had no fear of torture, pain, suffering or death because his belief in the truth of this Christian faith overrode any superficial suffering he may have had. A man who knows so deeply what he believes and who he is, has no fear of anything this life can throw against him.

Life cannot be lived from an armchair, it must be confronted, wrestled and put in a headlock or do we just allow it to crash into us, being hospitalised again and again. Then we really are little more than crash victims.

- "Victims cry out 'The world is responsible for me' and then never do anything to take charge of their lives." (Anonymous)

- "If it is never our fault, we cannot take responsibility for it. If we can't take responsibility for it, we will always be its victim." (Richard Ball)

- "There is always free cheese in the mouse trap but the mice there aren't happy." (Anonymous)

- "Adversity will break the weak and expose the strong." (Anonymous)

19

WORRY ABOUT YOURSELF

Australians report some of the highest rates in the world for dissatisfaction in life. We are in the midst of widespread problems with obesity, with depression and a full range of mental health issues. Our marriages are only holding together in around fifty percent of cases. We complain about lack of fulfilment at work. And on the home front we are more likely to be involved in road rage incidents, squabble in restaurants and argue about the behaviour of neighbours.

My grandmother was fond of telling me (if she thought I was distracted by outside things) 'worry about yourself, you have enough issues without concentrating on the actions of others.' Of course, she was correct and like all modern Australians I have nothing to worry about on a 'world scale.' Unlike her generation I have not known war. She endured both WWI and WWII, she lost two husbands, bought up four young girls by herself, worked cleaning houses throughout their young years, went through the great depression and never left the state of Victoria or owned a car. Yet, she still managed to live a contented and fruitful life.

Absolutely, I have nothing to complain about, but why do so many Australians feel so crippled by life? We live longer than previous generations, we have more education, more medical care, greater travel opportunities, an abundance of food, amusements, entertainment and wealth inconceivable to previous generations. Yet, we are a generation depressed, often jealous of others and with a severe lack of drive to achieve or undertake new things.

Australians are more 'protected' today. We have rights, but we are more easily offended, we are increasingly 'hurt' by the words or opinions of others and we are more likely to stay home watching movies on 'mental health days.' Australians are richer and benefit from greater wealth than at any time in our history, yet we appear to have lost something as well: the hard edge and the ability to fight for things at personal cost – yes – we can whinge, but do we fight to change much, even in our own lives?

In many ways Australians are crippled by their own perceptions and thinking. In my view there are two ways to make significant beneficial change to your own life and both begins with you.

Firstly, know the difference between being uncomfortable in life and crippling or life debilitating injuries. Most of us are only uncomfortable in life: our mechanical devices breakdown, I may be offended by someone. We may not get what we think we deserve. We may have been underpaid or been dealt shitty service but is any of this life threatening? No, it's not.

Very few of us face life threatening situations, very few will wake this morning in wheelchairs unable to walk. Few of us face years of painful rehabilitation from serious accidents. The great irony of this distinction is that those in the second situation are always striving to advance, to change, to walk again, to be the people they know themselves to be, so why have the rest of us stopped? If we are able to remind ourselves that none of these inconsequential issues actually derails life, then we are better placed to move forward with the real and significant questions and tasks of life.

The second focus is not to be distracted by what others have or are doing? Jealously is another failure of thinking and perception. If I am consumed with why another person drives a nice car, this focus is almost always on the immediate. What's important is the big picture. They may have worked seven days a week for many years to afford such a vehicle. It may have been purchased through an inheritance gift. It may be leased through a company arrangement. Just seeing the immediate, the person has a new car, fails to tell you anything and it fails to tell you the truth about your own 'big picture life.'

All of us has the potential in Australia to be wealthy and comfortable. The 'big picture' is that we will need to work for around 30 years to save consistently and to build our wealth steadily. Some of us will need to work a second job. Do this and Australian life will guarantee you wealth. The question is are you prepared to do it? As my grandmother would say, 'worry about yourself, you have enough issues without concentrating on the actions of others.'

- "Limits, like fear is an illusion." (Michael Jordan)

- "I have self-doubt. I have insecurity. When I show up for a game, my back hurts and my feet are sore. I don't deny it, I embrace it." (Kobe Bryant)
- "Jealously is only fear." (Anonymous)
- "We can easily forgive a child who is afraid of the dark, the real tragedy is when men are afraid of the light." (Plato)
- "It is not death that man should fear, but he should fear never beginning to live." (Anonymous)

20

THE IMMATURITY OF FEELING OFFENDED

Modern Australia is an intellectual environment where many people are afraid to actually say what they really think. In my view this is a great regret, as intellectual ideas, and the development of our own way of thinking needs to be tested against the ideas of others. In a healthy society the public arena should be a place where free discussion reigns.

At Mission Engage we value and uphold all sorts of ideas, even ones that I don't like! but be warned you will be certainly get an argument in return. In my view, none of this is disrespectful, its one important way we grow in maturity and ultimately in value to our society.

Increasingly we hear people suggest that some ideas should not be spoken in public. These ideas may be controversial, and they may concern people who are also on our courses. Respect and gentle argument are healthy ways of learning from each other. Mature individuals don't go around offending others for the sake of it, but there is nothing wrong with having an opinion and being prepared to argue for it.

At Mission Engage we do have a lot to say to you, we talk

about your public presentation, the way you communicate, your confidence and how to make yourself a better person. In the same way others are free to express their ideas to me. I am a Catholic Priest, people have many viewpoints that challenge my positions, if I were to be offended that would be my problem and I am free to defend my position with rational argument.

At Mission Engage we encourage young Australians to have their say, but we don't accept sulking and quitting because someone else holds a different view. If you are offended by the views of others, then that responsibility for maturity lies with you.

Mission Engage is an environment where you are free and safe to express ideas and views, sadly, there is an ever-decreasing number of places in Australia where it is safe to do so. Therefore, there will be fewer and fewer places in Australia where you can engage in discussion with someone you disagree with.

At Mission Engage we are opposed to a society that promotes grievance against each other for what we think. We challenge individuals who may feel insulted by other members of our society who have a different viewpoint from their own. Surrounding people with legal regulations to protect them from alternative ideas is not in our view a way into a healthy future.

As New York columnist Brett Stephens pointed out on his recent tour of Australia, 'there is an art to disagreement and every great idea is really just a spectacular disagreement with some other great idea. If you don't challenge each other with ideas how will we ever know the truth.'

- "I disapprove of what you say but I will defend to death your right to say it." (Voltaire)
- "If liberty means anything at all, it means the right to tell people what they do not want to hear." (George Orwell)
- "If freedom of speech is taken away then dumb and silent we may be led, like sheep to the slaughter." (George Washington)
- "Hypocrites get offended by the truth." (Jess C Scott)
- "Whoever would overthrow the liberty of a nation must begin by subduing the freeness of speech." (Benjamin Franklin)

21

YOUR CULTURE

Australians are rightly proud of the contribution that migrant communities have made to Australian life. The migration of many people of differing backgrounds, languages and cultures has enriched the Australian community for many decades. Many migrants bring a proud history of hard work, strong family and community values and an outstanding desire to succeed. If you belong to one of these immigrant communities you should be rightly proud of their contribution to Australian life.

Nevertheless, there is an even more important cultural contribution to Australian life: that is your personal culture. This is the culture you bring to Australia every day.

This culture, your personal culture, is witnessed in your actions and behaviours every day of the week, by everyone you meet. Your personal culture is one of the most important things you own and will largely determine your success or otherwise in the world – particularly in the workplace. Disappointingly, many Australians imagine that their behaviours and actions are not seen by others or have the rather strange view that others must accept their actions and behaviours at face value.

The mantra, that this is 'who I am' and that others must accept me with warts and all, is the mantra of a failing individual. The truth is vastly different, no one has to accept anything about you and people will quickly determine whether you are a person they wish to know or include in their lives!

The difficulty for individuals who imagine that others must 'adapt' to them is that they have forgotten that actions and behaviours are 'matters of choice'. When we understand that our 'culture' towards other is a matter of choice, then we can appreciate the value of being our best for others. The world is full of 'mediocre' people who do not bring excellence to their personal interactions with others. These are the people who cannot be bothered to acknowledge others, who cannot pause to say good morning or to enquire about another person's life, these are the individuals who disrespect others by being late and not fulfilling the tasks they said they would do. These are the people who constantly expect you to adapt to their needs but have little concept of 'doing' something for others without it being seen as a significant burden. Don't make the mistake of imagining that these behaviours are not seen or taken note of!

If we are able to develop a personal culture in excellence is all that we do the possibility of impacting creatively and pastorally in people lives is dramatically increased. A word of encouragement, a small act of generosity, a willingness to share a burden of others can make a profound difference to the lives of other. And all it requires of us is small amount of time and the ability to 'see' others.

Offering to help someone with a small job or driving another to an appointment are opportunities to transform the lives of others. When you don't take these things lightly you are offering others an 'extraordinary culture' and in your own way impacting and making the world a better place. You don't need to 'do' great things to be an extraordinary person, you just need to bring excellence into the ordinary things of life that most of us overlook.

Most Australians will tell you they are trying to improve their lives, and so we study, undertake courses and seek out mentors. At Mission Engage, we think one small change can give even greater benefits. Your personal culture of excellence, your generosity of time and interest in others will far outweigh all that you can learn in study and the difference to others will be even more profound.

- "And he looked up and saw the rich putting their gifts into the treasury, and he saw a poor widow putting in two coins. So, he said, truly I say to you, this widow has put in more than all these who out of their abundance have put in offerings for God, but she out of her poverty has put in all that she had." (Jesus Christ)
- "No one is useless in this world who lighten the burden of others." (Charles Dickens)
- "We make a living by what we get, we make a life by what we give." (Winston Churchill)
- "For it is in giving that we receive." (Francis of Assisi)

22

TAKE THE LONG WAY HOME

Theodore Roosevelt Jr was an American statesman and 26th President of the United States from 1901-1909. He was born an unhealthy child with serious asthma and chest complaints, but he managed to overcome his physical restrictions by embracing an aggressive range of outdoor activities, including horse riding, hunting and boxing. Perhaps because of his unhealthy childhood, Roosevelt lived a successful life based on one of his most famous quotes, "Nothing in the world is worth having or worth doing unless it means effort, pain and difficulty…I have never in my life envied a human being who led an easy life. I have envied a great many people who led difficult lives and led them well."

Sadly, to our great cost as a nation this view of life is held to be truthful by very few Australians. In fact, many of us are attempting to do the exact opposite in most areas of our life. We are not generally a nation of 'slow builders' who work towards our goals and overcoming obstacles at a steady rate. We are a society of instant gratification, that is we see something we want, and we usually desire it immediately. The short-term view is usually our goal and we do this over and over again. Our credit card debt is the obvious proof of our burning desire to wait for nothing.

We are a nation of debt. Certainly, many people will have a long-term debt on a home usually undertaken over 30 years, but what about all the other stuff; will we wait for a new car, TV, computers, new release music, clothes, restaurants or an annual holiday? Not likely! Do we not bring all of these things into the immediate, all justified by some version of 'I deserve it?

Australians owed over 51 billion in credit card debt in 2016, twenty years earlier, our total debt was 5 billion on credit cards. The average debt on a credit card is around $4,200 per person, perhaps, you say that doesn't sound too much yet only 10% of individuals pay off their card balances each month, over half will only make the minimum payment required, which just means we continue in debt month after month. A $2,000 debt takes 12 years to repay, if we are to only repay the minimum repayment. During those 12 years our total repayments would be almost 3 times what we borrow.

When it comes to work, life, family, relationships or learning, at Mission Engage we value a slow, deliberate and concentrated build, its not important you get the house finished in a week, it is important you build a secure concrete slab on which to build. The foundation of what you build are more important than a mad rush to complete things, only to find they don't work or are poorly constructed.

The great difference between Australians who are rich and those who are poor, is that rich ones are able to delay gratification, that is, they are prepared to wait. Rich people recognise credit card debt as a form of poverty put off for years into the future but still a poverty that will arrive!

At Mission Engage we encourage participants to peel off the unnecessary and the inconsequential. This is one of the keys to a successful life. And yes, cut up those cards!

- "Don't give up what you want for what you want now." (Richard C Scott)
- "If you don't want to be average, don't rush into what the crowd is doing." (Constance Friday)
- "Without delayed gratification, there is no self-control." (Sunday Adelaja)

23

FROM DEVOTEE TO DISTINCTION

We live in a world where many of our fellow citizens are contented to be followers of others. In Australia we have fans for every conceivable individual, club or group. We have followers of sports stars, we have celebrity chefs with thousands of adoring fans, we have football supporters in their millions, who claim allegiance to a particular club. We even have individuals like the Kardashians who have millions of followers without appearing to have any particular skills, insights or wisdom!

At Mission Engage we don't advocate for life as a fan. We advocate for a much more authentic form of life, one that is clearly shaped and defined by you. We promote and support a life that is based on substance beyond any superficial outward appearances. Where the central core is to be found in personal freedom, speaking what's on your mind and making choices that benefit both you and importantly those around you. This is not an easy path to undertake, but making a distinct life is a task in which all humans are called to engage.

At Mission Engage, we believe that those who choose to ignore life's challenges and difficulties do indeed suffer consequences of loss of self-esteem, lack of identity and drive and lack of self-fulfilment. We consider these consequences to be intolerable. At Mission Engage we accept that many aspects of life will be uncomfortable, that sometimes we will need to take unpopular stands and that a full life involves regular failure. Nevertheless, it is only through a life clearly shaped by values owned by us that we will develop character, forget the immaturity of insignificant things and undertake distinct lives.

At Mission Engage we recognise the distinctions of life as shown by individuals such as Winston Churchill, Margaret Thatcher, Albert Jacka, Max Kolbe and Abraham Lincoln. We do not hold these people as perfect or even mostly successful, but as full expressions of authenticity and worth. That task we are all challenged to undertake, "for to humanity to whom much is given much is expected".

ABOUT THE AUTHOR

Fr James Grant MAICD BA BTh GDip IS GDip Comp ST GDip Trauma Counselling

Born in Adelaide, and schooled in Essendon, Victoria. Fr James joined the Commonwealth Police in 1977 with an initial posting in Canberra. He has qualified as a martial arts instructor in Brazilian Jiu Jitsu, scuba diving and played first grade cricket for Northcote.

Fr James undertook theological studies at Melbourne University, graduating in 1984. Appointed to the UK as an associate priest, He became one of London's first white vicars to minister to the expanding West Indian community Fr James initiated his first interfaith gatherings in west London following the Brixton riots, after which he was appointed on short term placement to Berlin (west Germany) in 1988 and Budapest in 1989.

Fr James returned to Australia in 1989 where he was Senior Chaplain at Geelong Grammar School for seven years, followed by two years at St Michael's grammar and six years at The Peninsula School. He was noted for his pastoral care with a focus on martial arts, football and cricket as methods for building confidence in students.

In 2004 he was appointed a parish priest at St Stephens Richmond, then in 2005 Melbourne's first team vicar for the new parish of Jika Jika in Melbourne's north with responsibility for a large Sudanese refugee community. As Parish priest for the Preston area, he was a strong advocate for the Nuba people, of Sudan, who are experiencing genocide. He has built two schools in Northern India.

Fr James founded Chaplains Without Borders in 2004 to initiate new ventures into corporate and community organisations, and CWB grew to be Australia's largest chaplaincy service within 2 years. He went on to be appointed as the world's first chaplain to the casino industry in 2006 (Crown Enterprises Australia) a position he still retains.

As a leading traditionalist within the Australian church, Fr James supported the development to the Anglican Ordinariate in Australia and served on the national committee as secretary 2010-2011. Fr James was received into the Catholic Church and ordained as a Catholic Priest in September 2012 as a foundational priest for the Australian Ordinariate. In 2012 he was appointed National director for Ordinariate schools and to the Ordinariate governing council.

Fr James has continued to develop missions including Catholics in Business 2012 and Catholics in Mission and renewal in 2013. His CYA (Catholic Youth Academy) youth program works through Crown casino to develop confidence in de-motivated young Australians and find work placements within Crown. In 2013 he co-established the Renewal Centre.

He is the first Chaplain appointed to an A league soccer club in Australia at the largest Australian club, Melbourne Victory. He is involved with 9MM and 45ACP pistol competition and is completing PPL training for Helicopters

In 2015 Fr James established the Father James Grant foundation, implementing programs for de-motivated young Australians. The "mission Engage" program has now helped around 300 young Australians find their first Job. The Resurgence Group is a team designed to help parishes re-energize their community life.

Web:
www.chaplainswithoutborders.org
www.catholicsinbusiness.org
www.thefatherjamesgrantfoundation.org
www.resurgence.org

www.ingramcontent.com/pod-product-compliance
Lightning Source LLC
Chambersburg PA
CBHW071851230426
43671CB00012B/2144